Emotional B
Understanding /
With Manipulative People
Like A Pro

Antony Felix

Introduction

If you do not do this, then I will (threat). You are the reason why this is happening (blame). Because you don't pay attention to my needs (guilt trip)...

Have you heard these kinds of statements repeatedly from someone? For some reason, you seem to be the one who is doing something to them and you have been the only one apologizing, and the one to make sacrifices, going an extra mile to make them comfortable – to try to make things better between you. You are made to feel vulnerable and answerable to them, yet you know that is not the 'normal' order of the relationship.

I know they made you feel like you were crazy and over reactive when you called them out on their behavior, pushing you around to do what they want. At some point, you may have felt that they were right and you were irrational. But that's how a manipulative person works to break their victim's defenses.

Now, we have a name for this kind of behavior; emotional blackmail. If you have been through such then you have been emotionally blackmailed. Sadly, it's not done by strangers; it is common within some of our valued relationships with people closest to us such as friends, partners and even parents.

It is not easy to identify when you are being manipulated this way, especially if it happens with someone you love.

However, regardless of who the perpetrator is, emotional manipulation will hurt you and steal your life and happiness.

Lucky for you though, this book provides insights on this behavior, to teach you how to recognize it and also how to deal with it and end it. The book will help you grow a spine so that you can take your life back!

Your Free Gift

As a way of thanking you for the purchase, I'd like to offer you a complimentary gift:

- **5 Pillar Life Transformation Checklist:** This short book is about life transformation, presented in bit size pieces for easy implementation. I believe that without such a checklist, you are likely to have a hard time implementing anything in this book and any other thing you set out to do religiously and sticking to it for the long haul. It doesn't matter whether your goals relate to weight loss, relationships, personal finance, investing, personal development, improving communication in your family, your overall health, finances, improving your sex life, resolving issues in your relationship, fighting PMS successfully, investing, running a successful business, traveling etc. With a checklist like this one, you can bet that anything you do will seem a lot easier to implement until the end. Therefore, even if you don't continue reading this book, at least read the one thing that will help you in every other aspect of your life. Grab your copy now by clicking/tapping here or simply enter http://bit.ly/2fantonfreebie into your browser. Your life will never be the same again (if you implement what's in this book), I promise.

PS: I'd like your feedback. If you are happy with this book, please leave a review on Amazon.

Table of Contents

Introduction _____ 2

Your Free Gift _____ 4

Recognizing Emotional Blackmail; What Does It Look Like? _____ 8

    How It Works _____ 8

The Six Progressive Steps Of Blackmail ___ 11

Strategies Of Emotional Blackmail _____ 14

    How To Detect The Perpetrator _____ 16

    Characteristics Of An Emotional Blackmailer __ 17

    Personalities Likely To Use Emotional Blackmail _____ 20

Are You A Victim? _____ 23

4 Common Types Of Emotional Blackmail 26

    Patterns That Point To Emotional Blackmail In A Relationship _____ 29

Disclaimer _____ 31

    Pointers of a genuine and appropriate demand 32

Strategies To Stop Emotional Blackmail And Take Your Life Back _____ 36

1: Change Your Mindset 36
   Change The Way You Think About Yourself; Raise Your Self-Esteem 37
   How To Raise Your Self-Esteem And Feel Secure In Your Own Skin 38
   Change Your Perception About Relationships _ 41
   How To Overcome Emotional Neediness 44

Cultivate Mental Resilience 47
   What Does It Mean To Be Mentally Resilient?_ 47
   6 Ways To Cultivate Mental Resilience............ 49

Develop Boundaries **54**
   Signs Of Lack Of Or Weak Boundaries 55
   How To Establish Boundaries 56
   How To Make Your Boundaries Stand 59

How To Handle A Blackmail Situation And The Blackmailer In The Moment **63**
   Non-Defensive Communication Skills 64
   Additional Tips In Handling Blackmail On The Spot 65

The Final Card **67**

Conclusion **68**

Do You Like My Book & Approach To Publishing? _____ **69**

   1: First, I'd Love It If You Leave a Review of This Book on Amazon._____ 69

   2: Check Out My Emotional Mastery Books ___ 69

   3: Grab Some Freebies On Your Way Out; Giving Is Receiving, Right? _____ 70

Recognizing Emotional Blackmail; What Does It Look Like?

Emotional blackmail is a tactic commonly used by people we let close to us, to hurt and manipulate us to serve their agendas. They could be using it intentionally or unintentionally – some people just don't know another way to get their way. However, intentional or not, this form of manipulation has an undertone; if you do not comply with my wants, you will suffer.

As harmless as it may look, as many perpetrators are termed as just being 'bossy' or 'pushy' not to mention that they can be really sweet to their victims after getting what they want, this behavior is harmful.

It is a form of psychological abuse which intends to control the victim's decision making ability and behavior through unhealthy ways, and it causes damage to the victim, emotionally, psychologically and mentally.

Being subjected to this kind of blackmail can affect the way a person sees themselves, causing their self esteem to fall and losing their confidence and sense of worth.

How It Works

The perpetrator places demands and threats on a victim. They shift blame and responsibility of their own negative actions to them and create feelings of fear, guilt and obligation so that the victim is pushed into doing what the abuser wants.

Therefore, in order for emotional blackmail to occur, these four must be present:

- *A demand* – They forcefully ask for something that the victim does not want to/is not prepared to give. They make a demand in order to get the upper hand where their interests are conflicting.

  Usually, the demand is something the victim considers unreasonable or unfair but the perpetrator does not care what they feel or think – they know they can get it by applying the right amount of pressure. It becomes a vicious cycle of manipulation as the blackmailer has already mastered just how much pressure it takes to get their victim to comply.

- *The threat* – the victim is made aware of the consequences they will face if they refuse to give in to the blackmailer's demands. Usually, it's something that is going to hurt the victim directly or affect someone or something they hold dear negatively.

  It could be about damaging a reputation, a valued object, a relationship or an agreement. For instance, they may threaten to end a relationship with the victim or tell their secret(s). In other cases, the consequence may be the blackmailer threatening to harm themselves if they know that the victim cares too much to let that happen.

- *The blackmailer* – This is the person fighting for control over another person with demands and threats as ammunition. Some of them do it intentionally while others are completely unaware of the hurt they are causing their victim. They just can't help themselves as they know no other way to get what they want.

- *The victim* – For emotional blackmail to take place, there has to be a willing victim. By a 'willing victim', we mean a person who is willing to sacrifice their values, principles and boundaries to give in to the demands in order to escape the consequences.

The Six Progressive Steps Of Blackmail

When the manipulator wants to take advantage of their victim, it all starts so well – and it's too smooth that you will not know you are being blackmailed. However, it's a pattern with six recognizable steps. We are going to discuss them below; if you notice the first three go down with a person, then you should know what they are trying to do (to use your emotions against you) and take the necessary measure to abort their mission.

This is how a single blackmail episode occurs:

i. *The demand*: The demand is usually followed by a threat. Why not ask nicely, without threats? It's because they have studied the victim. They know them and they know that their demand will not be received well; they know it's unreasonable. The threat is meant to drive the point home – to make it clear that the victim should not refuse.

ii. *Victim resistance*: The second step is the expected resistance from the victim. They attempt to push back; they resist and maybe try to avoid this person who is making unreasonable demands with threats since they do not know how to handle the situation. They know that what they are being asked is unfair or against their values but also, there is a threat (consequences) to think about. They make an attempt to push back hoping to be left alone which pushes the blackmailer to take step three.

iii. *Applying pressure*: The manipulator won't leave without getting what they want. This is the step where they apply pressure on the victim. You see, they have no qualms about pushing too hard or hurting the victim, their goal is to get their way, it does not matter what they have to do.

This is the part where they will accuse the victim of being crazy or irrational. They will find reasons to put blame on them or take them on a guilt trip if this is what it takes. If just the right buttons are pushed with this pressure, the victim starts to question their sense of reality and lose touch with the healthy sense of perspective and stop listening to their gut. Confusion sets in and they get vulnerable.

iv. *Threats*: More pressure is applied with threats with the intention of pushing the victim over the edge. They make the victim aware of the consequences they face if they fail to comply. Usually, they will create a situation, which makes the victim responsible for any negative outcomes. For instance, "Your refusal to do this for me, will be the reason I might go looking for someone else".

v. *Victim compliance*: No one wants to be responsible for bad things happening to them or someone they love, especially if you are the person who cares too much and take things personally. The victim, who probably has such characteristics, will believe the threats and give in to pressure.

vi.   *Retreat and repeat*: The blackmailer gets their way: they will get what they want and withdraw temporarily, and maybe completely ignore or play nice to the victim until their next want comes up.

Strategies Of Emotional Blackmail

There are three common strategies used by the emotional blackmailer, commonly referred to as FOG. It is important to note that they could either use one or a combination of the three – whatever gives you a good enough push to submit to them.

The strategies are usually made of strong emotions that make you tick. They include:

- *Fears*

Fear is a strong emotion built to protect us from danger. It is that feeling we experience when we anticipate that something will hurt us or something bad will happen to a loved one. Whenever you sense danger, this feeling will arise so that you can withdraw and take measures to stay out of harm's way; you will run, avoid, beg, submit, change tactic, whatever it takes to stay safe.

Manipulators will use this emotion to oblige you to give in to their demand. Given that this person is close to you and that they know you too well, they will use your most dreaded fears against you, to get what they want.

Below are examples of fears commonly used by black mailers:

- Fear of abandonment
- Fear of conflict
- Fear of loss

- Fear of confrontation
- Fear of the unknown
- Fear of hurting loved ones

They know how terrified you are of say abandonment and you would do anything to keep them around. The threat will therefore be something like "do what I want lest I leave you", "I am going to end this relationship if you ask me about her again" and then you will back down because you want to keep them around – the manipulator knows that this is exactly how you will respond.

- *Sense of obligation*

The manipulator will make you feel obligated to do what they want – they press just the right buttons to make you feel like it's your duty to do it. They know exactly what techniques to use to make sure that you see yourself as a very bad, irresponsible or ungrateful person for refusing to let them have their way.

For instance, a manipulative partner will create a habit of coming home late in the night without a good explanation of where they were. When questioned about it, they claim that they have to stay out late to work so you can have all the luxuries you are enjoying – and they expect that you would understand, cut out the drama and be grateful. The victim will then feel that it's their duty to appreciate their partner for making the sacrifices and stop with the questions and concerns about the issue.

- *Guilt*

After being made to feel as if doing something is a duty, what follows is that you are made to feel guilty for not doing it. The perpetrator will make it seem as if we deserve to suffer for not doing what we are obligated to do.

For instance, in our example above, the manipulator may make the victim feel guilty for being asleep or relaxing at home while they toil away. They may even go as far as threatening to find a more appreciative partner to go home to, instead of coming home to questions and drama.

Mind you, it could be that their partner's concerns are valid since the manipulator could be getting home late due to something sinister he/she is doing and using blackmail to cover their tracks. This is what blackmailers do; they use blackmail as a cover up of something in them (insecurities, fear, low self-esteem) or something going on with them (lies, cheating, extortion). This brings us to our next point of discussion.

How can you identify an emotional blackmailer?

How To Detect The Perpetrator

If only they could have a scary face, then we would identify them instantly and stay as far away from them as we could. But no, these manipulators tend to have the sweetest faces and we are too close to them. In fact, we love them dearly – and even if they were pointed out by a fairy godmother to protect us, we still couldn't believe they would do that to us.

Hard as it to believe, these blackmailers are some of the closest people to us. This is how they know your emotional triggers and the right buttons to press to make you dance to whatever tunes they play.

Characteristics Of An Emotional Blackmailer

- A person who always reacts negatively to your choices – they want to manipulate your decisions and even though your choices may be right, they will make sure that you know they dislike them and use your need for approval/to please to make you follow their choices and then they will be happy.

- They are constantly blaming or accusing. Everything that goes wrong is your fault and even though you may not be directly involved in some issues, they still will find a way to connect you – and then subject you to some guilt tripping.

- They want to dominate a conversation and their arguments are always on the right. They do not know how to listen and they are not flexible in accepting or just hearing out other people's opinions.

- They will not take advice, even if they need it. They consider it an abuse to their intelligence because they believe they know everything – and they can never go wrong.

- They can switch their moods from being on top of the world happy to raving mad in a matter of seconds. It is the same way they could treat you like royalty now and in a few minutes treat you like you are garbage.

Their mood (or how they treat you) depends on whether they are getting their way or not. If you resist their control, their character and mood fluctuates at an amazing speed. These are the type of people we say are giving us 'mixed signals' and we never really know where we stand with them.

- They want to be seen as the hero, the savior and the guy who is ahead of everyone. For this reason, they will often boast about their achievements, 'fabulous' lives and properties.

N.B: Beware of their vibes!

They emanate some unhealthy negative vibes that you are likely to pick up on especially if you are empath. When in front of them, your sensations will speak more than their words, even if their choice of vocabulary is the sweetest. If you listen to your emotions, you will feel like something is 'off' about them.

Note that, a healthy person will give off healthy vibes but an unhealthy person is likely to make us feel uncomfortable, frustrated, undecided and even unwell. Also, it is important to note that the mind also picks up on the negative energy of an unhealthy person, like the manipulator. It knows that something is wrong but then it is easy to convince that all is well as the fears, threats and emotions (such as love) to this person rise to invalidate the voice of doubt and reason.

However, even if you go against yourself to trust this person, there will always be doubt and a weird uncomfortable feeling in the background, which tells you that 'this is not right'. If this voice and feelings are constantly against person, chances are they may be the manipulators in your circle, controlling you and taking away the life you are supposed to be living.

Personalities Likely To Use Emotional Blackmail

Watch out for people with these personalities, as they are more likely to use this type of psychological manipulation to have things their way. Beware of;

i. *The loud and dramatic*

Have you encountered this type of people who are so loud and do not shy away from creating drama anywhere, anytime. They will create a mountain out of a mole hill and make so much fuss about a small issue.

The problem with this type is that they are insecure with themselves and thus they will try everything to look for significance and approval. They will use blackmail to make their partners pay attention to them and to feel guilty for their instability.

ii. *The narcissist*

This type believes that they are the best in everything and they deserve to get the best of everything even at the cost of other people's suffering. In a nutshell, the narcissist does not give a hoot about anyone else's needs but theirs.

Blackmail is their best tool to intimidate and undermine people, to put down any conflicting decisions or ideas so that theirs can stand out. They tend to use people to further their selfish agendas. What better way to do this than to use the FOG strategy of blackmail?

iii. The critic

There is nothing wrong with being critical; we all need some level of criticism, to correct us since we don't get everything right. However, there are some people who take this too far being overly critical with the intention of undermining others. They will make a person believe that they are not doing enough or being good enough at something all in an effort to influence their behavior so as to get to control outcomes. Usually, they do this for situations that they feel are out of their hands; it's their way of gaining the upper hand by using intimidation and blackmail.

iv. The passive aggressive

These are hostile people in nature but they are not direct with expressing their hostility. For instance, they will not beat you or kick you out of the house. Instead, they will use indirect ways such as stubbornness, insults or fail you deliberately.

They are unable to communicate straightforwardly and thus they will turn to mechanisms such as emotional manipulation or sarcasm to get you to do what they want.

v. The insecure/low self-esteem individual

This type has a deep rooted fear of not being worthy or good enough. For instance, they do not believe that they are worthy of love or attention and thus they have to do something in order to get it.

Often they result to emotional blackmailing to make up for their insecurities and low sense of worth. They will use it to make you feel guilty of their insecurities and get your attention fully focused on them – or else. They will manipulate your emotions to make you feel inadequate so that they can feel powerful. This type of people will use whatever technique to bring you down and take you on numerous guilt trips, even feign hurt just to get your attention.

Are You A Victim?

It is not enough to be aware of the likely faces of the blackmailer. It is equally important to know they type of people who are targeted; the victim. You see, perpetrators are everywhere but they know whom to target; they have ways of identifying the people who can take their BS. Are you a likely target?

Let's look at some common characteristics of the blackmail victim; character traits that sell them out to the manipulator.

i. Having a strong sense of responsibility; these are the kind of people who will not let anything go wrong if they can help it. They feel responsible for everyone and everything and they will make insane sacrifices just to fix things. That's why the manipulator will use guilt and obligation to get to them.

ii. The one who has a strong desire to please; if you are the kind that will do anything to please people, you can be blackmailed easily. They know you are afraid of disappointing them or anyone for that matter. That's why they will use a secret of yours against you – threatening to tell and disappoint say, your parents.

iii. The polite human who loves peace and fears confrontations. Your fear will be used against you; they know you do not want to get into an argument and thus they can threaten drama – or cause it to make you stop standing up for your values/standards/rights and give in.

iv. The empath – the one who connects with and understands the emotions of others. They will play the role of a victim to get you where they want.

v. The emotionally dependent – If you depend on others for the stability of your emotions, you area in trouble. If you are happy when they are happy, you will do what they want to please them so that you can be happy too.

vi. Love addicted – you cannot stand not being in love. They will know to threaten you with ending the relationship and you will dance to their tune to keep the love.

vii. Low self-esteem – you do not think highly of yourself and therefore the blackmailer, a possible narcissist, will find you easy prey, to feed on your low self-esteem and use your vulnerability to feel strong.

viii. Weak sense of identity – since you cannot stand for who you are, they may as well tell you who to be and make it seem right.

ix. Lack of standards/values – This means that you have no rules in your life and no boundaries so anyone can walk in and mess with whatever they want and control you – and you will not even resist.

x. Co-dependency – entirely depending on people to be the source of your happiness, to pay your bills and so on makes you to be easily controlled. People will dump their agendas on you and you will have to take it because you need to keep them around you.

4 Common Types Of Emotional Blackmail

The blackmailer is likely to adopt any of the following roles, depending on their blackmail strategy, which is guided by their knowledge of your emotional triggers:

i. The long suffering victim

In this role, the manipulator assumes the role of a victim. They wear the misery as a crown, holding it over their victim's head to make them submit to their wants. Their suffering is made to be the fault of the victim.

They are suffering or in pain because of something the victim did or is doing. In other instances, they make their victim believe that they ought to do something for them failure to which they will cause them to suffer. Sometimes, they will expect that the other person figures out what's hurting or bothering them without being told; failure to which they are accused of not loving or caring for them enough.

The sufferer uses a combination of fear, guilt and obligation to get to their victims.

ii. The executer/punisher

This type of blackmailer does not mince their words when they tell about the consequences of not doing what they want. They know how to punish their victims; they know what hurts them the most and they won't hesitate to do it. For instance, if you depend on them financially, they will threaten to withdraw their financial assistance knowing it will paralyze your livelihood.

In this role, fear is used the most.

iii. The tantalizer

In this role, the manipulator plays the "carrot before the horse" game. You could have heard of this narrative where a horse rider holds a carrot over the horse's head, close enough for it to smell it but far enough to be out of reach. The horse will keep going, even run, thinking it could 'catch' the carrot, which it never does. However, it covers the distance intended unknowingly; it does what the rider wants. This is the game the tantalizer plays.

They will promise a reward, a very attractive one in that case – usually something that they know the victim really wants. They will ask you to do something in exchange of another thing (the reward) but usually, it's not a fair trade. What's more, it is very likely that they will never give the reward.

A good example is lovers who take advantage of their unsuspecting partner, making them do things to satisfy their selfish wants such as putting their name on property deeds, with a promise to share a lifetime together – but they end up only using them.

All three strategies of manipulation are likely to come into play here; (fear) the victim is made to be afraid of missing out on the reward. (Obligation) they feel obligated because this person asked in good faith and is even offering a reward.

(Guilt) if that does not work, then guilt will give the victim the final push; no one wants to have an 'I wish I had...then I would have gotten...'

iv. Self-punishers

In this role, the victim, usually a person who cares about them is put in a position where they have to choose between submitting to the demands and the blackmailer's wellbeing. They will threaten to harm or punish themselves knowing all too well that it hurt the other person.

A good example for this would be a person threatening to commit suicide if a partner leaves them or even a person who claims that the victim's actions are causing them to be ill or suffer.

The main strategy of the self-punisher is guilt (they won't be able to live with it if their loved one follows through with the threat, say to harm themselves, so they think letting them have their way is far much easier to bear) but fear also comes into play. Since the victim is known to care about them, the blackmailer knows that they will be afraid of the fact that they will come to harm.

Most manipulators will use any of the three strategies and fall in the 4 categories discussed above. However, it is no guarantee that they will stick to just one; some of them will use a combination of all or switch between the four, to push all your buttons until you give in.

As mentioned earlier, it is hard to recognize it when you are being emotionally blackmailed because of this FOG that the perpetrators create in your mind. You will think they are genuine and that what they are doing is a normal part of the friendship or relationship but they are undercover manipulators. If you cannot notice the character traits, which they may be smart enough to hide, look out for the following patterns in your relationship with them; as they say, patterns don't lie;

Patterns That Point To Emotional Blackmail In A Relationship

- You are constantly made to feel as if you are crazy just for voicing your opinions and concerns.

- If one person is the one frequently apologizing for things they are not responsible for. For instance; having to apologize for things like the other person's bad mood or negative behavior

- One person makes all the decisions. Things are done their way or they are not done at all – even at the expense of the other person.

- Obedience is not done at will. One person is always intimidated, insulted or threatened to compliance.

- If sacrifices and compromises are to be made, it is always one person who has to do it all the time.

- If one person is made to feel selfish time and again for wanting something –or having a different opinion.

- Unreasonable demands that do not sit well with one person are made to seem reasonable with excuses and justifications.

- When one person's needs seem non-existent and concerns are ignored.

The blackmail game never ends; it's a vicious cycle. It does not matter how frequent the victim is exposed to such behavior. Whether it is one incident a month or on a daily basis, the truth about manipulation is that it has a negative effect on the victim – and the relationship. As a victim, you should not excuse the behavior just because it does not happen frequently. Actually, take note from the very first incident, and take measures to end it, because that one occurrence is enough to put this toxic cycle in place and to set a foundation for the pattern to continue.

Disclaimer

Not all demands are a sign of blackmail

It is important to understand that there are genuine demands or requests and there are demands intended for blackmail – you must be able to differentiate the two. You see, in any relationship, every individual has needs or wants different from the other person (s). Just because they want their needs considered or met, does not mean that they are trying to blackmail you.

Check for consistency of behavior

You can always tell by how they ask – and if they are being mean, is it consistent? We are human and sometimes our emotions get the best of us and we overreact and make threats and unreasonable demands. Also, we all have a degree of narcissism in us, the one that drives us to watch out for our interests in a world where everyone is pursuing their own.

Not every demand is blackmail. But also, there is a very thin line between genuine demands in a relationship whether with a friend, parent or lover and emotional blackmail – given that emotional attachment is involved.

Now that you have read this, it could be that you are labeling everyone close to you who has made you to do things you did not want to do as a manipulator. Mind you sometimes, we do not want to do things we are supposed to do. For instance, you may not be paying attention to your partner and they have asked you to find a way to spend time together or just end the relationship altogether because it has come dysfunctional.

Is this blackmail?

Now, before you go ahead and mess up your relationships and label everyone that loves you as a manipulator, because they are asking you to do stuff, let's look at some marks of genuine demands to guide you in your decision of whether they are manipulating you or not –nor whether you are blackmailing someone or not.

Pointers of a genuine and appropriate demand

i. When addressing an issue with someone behavior or actions, the focus is on the specific behavior or act and not on attacking someone's personality.

For instance, you don't say, "How can you do such a thing? You are such a selfish person!"

Instead, if they are doing something that is bothering you, which you think is selfish, a statement meant to address only your concern – without undermining someone should look like this example;

"You are always on your phone while we have a conversation, I feel like you are not listening to me and it hurts."

ii. When there is room for negotiations: A genuine demand should be open such that the other party can be able to say what they think, or if they agree to the terms.

iii. There ought to be realistic and appropriate consequences. Also, they should be consistently acted upon; otherwise, they will be interpreted as empty threats just to push a person to do something.

For example, don't say "I will not spend any time with you unless you help me with the dishes"

This would sound better "If you won't help with the dishes then I will not have enough time or energy to spend time together."

iv. Everybody's choices and opinions matter. One ought to be willing to accept the other person's choice/opinion without the blames or fear and they agree to face the consequences with integrity.

For example: In a relationship, when one feels like they are not compatible with the other party, they should be able to end it and walk away to nurse a heartbreak without blaming the other person or threatening them.

v. Emotions, needs, wants and requests are communicated clearly without blaming anyone or taking them on a guilt trip.

For example, instead of "We are growing apart because you don't care to spend time with me".

This will get you results without having to fight to gain control; "It's possible you do not know this but I really love and value time spent with you, just us"

vi. If they clearly express their needs and ask for things because something is important to them, without making it sound like a universal need or right.

"You are supposed to be doing this for me" is blackmail but a statement such as "I feel loved when you do this for me" is an appropriate request.

By now, you should have an idea of what emotional blackmail looks like. Do you think that you have been or continue to be a victim? It may be that you thought it was 'tough love" , a normal part of relationships or you have resigned yourself to suffer at the hands of the manipulator because 'they are just like that" and you chose to understand.

Whatever your case is, it is important to understand that emotional blackmail is toxic and it will steal your happiness and your life if it hasn't already. Imagine living a life where someone else is holding the reigns; you never get to be yourself and worse you can't help it because they are using emotions to make you dance to whatever tune they play like a string puppet. No matter how much you love them, no relationship is worthy having to live life on edge, limited and manipulated.

It is possible to shake off emotional blackmail. You deserve to live a beautiful life – on your terms, and you shouldn't take blame for other people's suffering and mistakes. You have already identified emotional blackmail; you can able to spot it. The next part of this book is dedicated to teaching you how to stand your ground, shake off the blackmailer and take your life back.

Read on.

Strategies To Stop Emotional Blackmail And Take Your Life Back

There is little you can do to make anyone change their habits – imagine how hard it is to even make yourself change yours. Therefore, trying to make the blackmailer change is more often than not, futile.

The only person you are going to succeed in changing is yourself; working on yourself is the best way to utilize your energy. Remember we talked about the characteristics of a victim, which make them more susceptible to blackmail?

Those make you so attractive to that villain. You need to change a few things that you need to change; to empower yourself so that you can resist the influence of this overbearing manipulative person (s) in your life. They include:

1: Change Your Mindset

Mindset refers to the state of mind; the way we think or the way our mind is programmed in a way that directs our ideas, thoughts and actions. As discussed in the previous part, if you are a victim of blackmail, chances are; you have traits or do certain things that make you vulnerable. Just to name but a few, there is low self-esteem and lack of self-worth all of which translate to thinking lowly of yourself.

Also, there is the need for validation, craving to be affirmed which makes you overlook yourself and your needs and go to painful lengths to please people. Why would anyone do that?

If you look closely, you will find that they don't think much of themselves; they do not know or think they are enough or worthy and thus need people to constantly affirm them, telling them they are important, beautiful, smart, worthy. They will do anything for it – manipulators really do love these ones. So how can you change your mindset to a way that makes you unattractive to manipulators? Let's discuss some points:

Change The Way You Think About Yourself; Raise Your Self-Esteem

You are an important part of this universe. You are beautiful, intelligent and worthy. You are a wonderful person and you deserve to be happy and to be loved. No one can say these words better than you; say them to yourself – think this about yourself.

You have been walking around and speaking to people with slouched shoulders, eyes cast down, fidgeting and biting your tongue as if you are a lesser human being. You have been acting as if you do not deserve to be present. Many times, you have tried to speak louder and walk a little taller but in this fake confidence, you still feel small and insignificant outside. People have found it easy to put you down and make you feel small.

Lack of confidence in yourself has caused you to become friends with people who are not good for you – and most of them are manipulators, using you and taking you for all you have. They make you feel good about yourself with their little praises and fake affection but they are taking more from you than you realize. You probably know or someone has mentioned that you are being used but you are thinking to yourself, "I have to keep them. They make me feel good sometimes" "I am no good. Who else would be interested to be friends with me?"

Maybe you have tried being with other people and being happy as you see other confident people but it never lasts long. It's not that you are not good enough. Stop dropping your self esteem that low and work on your perception of self. Have a sense of worth and realize that you are enough, just the way you are. You just need a different mindset – because no one on this planet will ever make you feel worthy if you can't see it yourself.

How To Raise Your Self-Esteem And Feel Secure In Your Own Skin

- *Program your subconscious mind to perceive you as good enough*

The subconscious mind is a deeper lying part of the human mind. It is the archive storing information for everything you have read, seen and experienced. By using this information, it shapes our beliefs and determines our outlook on life. You cannot delete what is already stored; you can only change the information you are storing now to change the narrative it tells you.

The best way to program your subconscious is using repetition; telling it the same story over and over again until it becomes a belief.

You can do this by:

- *Using affirmations*

They are simple positive statements that you repeat to yourself regularly so that your mind masters them and engraves them in your subconscious mind such that a belief is created – and is projected outward to bring that reality into existence. At face value, an affirmation can seem shallow or even stupid but repeat it enough times and see that you start to believe it.

For instance, for your self-esteem, wake up every day and say "I am special and unique. I am allowed to be different and still I am enough" "I let go of the belief that another person has to give me the love I need. I am my source of love". "I am smart and creative, nothing is impossible". You can create more affirmations that speak to your circumstances or fears. They need to focus on the positive regardless of how bad things are. They will help create a positive mindset, which is the first step towards changing your reality for the better.

- *Placing yourself in a favorable environment*

You have to be somewhere where what you trying to do is being supported. This is no to say that everyone should be telling you that you are good enough or something. However, there has to be less people critiquing you, undermining you or repeating the story of how you used to be. If they cannot affirm or encourage you, at least be around people who will let you become your best self while staying out of your business.

- Embracing positive self-talk

What narratives do you tell you about yourself? Did you know that they play a role in shaping your perceptions and realities? Most of us are victims of being our own worst critics, judging and condemning ourselves so harshly but we are out there trying to 'give the benefit of a doubt" and understanding other people. If only we could do that for ourselves...

Talk to yourself positively to attract a positive mentality about self. When you have this mentality, you tend to be more appreciative of yourself. You will not say "I messed up in my last relationship. I am not good enough for anyone". Instead, you are more likely to tell yourself "I made a lot of mistakes in my relationship but I sure have taken great lessons to become better at love". In this case, you are not likely to settle for a bad relationship with someone who is manipulating you. When you know you are better, you know you deserve better and you trust that you can find it.

What does self-esteem has to do with handling blackmail?

When you have a healthy self-esteem and a sense of worth:

- You value yourself and are comfortable and secure in your own skin. You do not need validations or someone to define who you are; you know who you are and what you want and thus you cannot be easily put down – or manipulated.

- o You know your worth and respect yourself. You do not bend over to please people at your own expense.

- o You are able to build healthy and extraordinary relationships

- o You are able to feel confident and stand your ground with your choices even if others will not approve of them. No one can force their choices or opinions on you.

- o You are comfortable in your own skin and do not compare yourself with others – or get undermined by their achievements. People will not make you feel bad for not measuring up to them or not being at a certain place in life.

- o In place of self-doubt and second-guessing yourself is unshakable confidence, you make firm decisions for your life and know you can achieve whatever you set your mind to. There is no room for people to impose their agendas on you.

Who would dare to control this kind of person, who knows who they are, what they want and is holding the reigns of their life this tight?

Change Your Perception About Relationships

What does being in a relationship with someone mean to you? It does not have to be a romantic relationship; friends and family are all people you share relationship with. Is it something that complements/adds to who you are or is it something that gives you your identity.

There is nothing wrong with enjoying the benefits of a relationship such as having someone to share love with, a person to lean on, having fun together and so on. However, when you come to rely on your relationships to be your source of happiness, validation, satisfaction and self-worth, such that you feel worthless and unhappy without it or the person, then there is a problem. It means you have lost your personal sense of identity.

Losing yourself in a relationship makes you needy which in turn makes you vulnerable and easy to take advantage of. Why is that? It is because you do not seem to have a life outside of the relationship and you have made these people to be the ones at the center of your life, controlling how you feel and what you do. You are dependent on them and thus they can twist and turn you however they want to get what they want. Woe unto you if you have a blackmailer in your circle.

Signs that you are emotionally needy and clingy in your relationships

- You often get emotionally overwhelmed and instantly 'need' your partner to reassure you and make you feel secure/better

- You look at your friends, family or partner to make you happy

- You are afraid that the people in your life are not there for you or have abandoned you. A call goes unanswered and a text not replied for a few minutes or an hour and you overreact, thinking that something is wrong – or wondering why they do not want to talk to you.

- You have an obsessive need to be in all their plans

- Your relationship is the center of your universe. If anything goes wrong with it, say a misunderstanding or a threat that the other person will not be there for you, everything in your world goes wrong.

- You look outside self for assurance and validation. You want them to tell you about your worth.

- You find it difficult to be alone- and when you are, you can't really focus on other things other than your partner. Instead of finding distractions, you will start to go over conversations with them, pinpointing things, like you were revising a book.

It's evident that being needy can make a very obsessive person, who does not know how to mind their own business. The manipulator finds this exciting and they will make sure that you have nothing else to mind other than their business. Since you need them so much, you won't be able to defend yourself as a threat will get you back in line, being their puppet.

There is a difference between being kind and loving and neediness. You can be a loving partner or friend without necessarily being needy. This gives you power not only to be a healthy partner in relationships but also to have a life and live it for you, without being controlled with emotional strings.

How To Overcome Emotional Neediness

- *Become aware of it:*

You need to recognize that there is a problem with the way you relate to or get attached to people. Look at your past and present relationships, and examine your feelings. Has there been a history of fear and anxiety? These questions will help you to identify and unhealthy relationship patterns that you may be ringing to your relationships. If the same negative feelings are always arising, chances are, you might have a problem. You know why? Because you just don't happen to meet people with similar annoying behaviors to cause you to react in the same type of way.

- Learn *to sit with your uncomfortable emotions and the uncertainties of life*

You will never be certain about everything in life. The truth is; life is full of things that you will never really understand and questions no one knows an answer to. Also, you will experience difficult emotions, which are pretty hard to deal with.

When this happens, instead of looking for a way to run away from them, seeking people to help you, sit with them. When you are experiencing anxiety over a situation or you have an impulse driven by emotions, to do something that you really are not sure you should do, sit with it; do not react. Watch and see what happens next if you do not react. Sitting with uncomfortable feelings helps keep you balanced both emotionally and mentally. It also keeps you from overwhelming people with constant attention seeking tendencies and nagging for them to fix your world.

- *Work on yourself*

When you examine your life and past and present experiences in relationships, what about you do you think you should improve? What has made you to be clingy in the past?

Maybe you do not feel confident; find ways to improve your self - esteem and feel more confident and comfortable in your own skin – and on your own. It could be that you did not have much going on for you in your life; now focus on doing things that you love. Pay attention to your hobbies and interests and dedicate time for them.

Look and identify areas of your life where you need to improve and do the work needed to make yourself better; a better person with a healthy self esteem and a better partner.

- *Have a life outside of your relationships*

It is healthy to have a full life outside of your relationships. This means that you just do not hang out with your partner, this one friend or members of your family all the time. Find activities to do other than those you do with them and spend time with other people. These are different sources of companionship distinct from your relationship so that you do not have to depend on one person/group.

Cultivate Mental Resilience

What Does It Mean To Be Mentally Resilient?

When you have mental resilience, in other words, you are mentally strong. The following are the privileges you get for having a strong mind:

- A resilient mind keeps you grounded such that you are not easily carried away by emotions to the point where you can't see logic or lose touch with reality or yourself. They will not get drunk with love to the point where they are getting blackmailed and refuse to see it.

  A mentally strong person will have relationships and friendships yes, but they are aware of what is happening – and they know when it's no longer a fair deal.

- It means that you are able to balance both negative and positive emotions in a way that works to your advantage - without leaning too much or getting carried away by either.

  You see, when you lean too much on the negative, you become a pessimist and when you get carried away by the positive, you get delusional and in both, you lose touch with the real world. When you are aware of both and you balance them just right, you can play the odds to work for you.

- You are able to keep your focus on the goal, without getting distracted by people or weighed down by circumstances. They are not lured by quick fixes promising instant gratification or discouraged for lack of approval by others. You know why? Their mind is set on their goals and they are aware of the process and are determined to do what it takes, regardless of people's opinions or how difficult it gets. No one can make you feel small or manipulate you with promises of too easy to get rewards.

6 Ways To Cultivate Mental Resilience

i.   Stop being in 'need', instead learn to just 'want'

Nobody walks around with an "I don't want to be liked, loved or approved" attitude. We all want to be liked; we all want love and to be approved or chosen by the people who matter to us.

This is not the problem.

Trouble is when we become in need of these things – in order to feel alright or complete and then we become devastated when we don't get them. A weak mind believes that they cannot function if they do not get the things they want – it's the end of the world for them.

A strong mind wants everything that everyone else wants; the good stuff that make us feel really good like love, approval, appreciation, a good life you name it. However, they do not attach their emotions to stuff like these, which can be here today and gone tomorrow. Apart from these things, they have a life and they can function perfectly well without.

It is being needy that makes you an easy target to manipulative people; it also makes it easy that they will get to you with their threats – mostly to deny you that which you are 'needing'.

Therefore, build a rich life of your own, where you are comfortable in who you are and what you have. If it's about love, cultivate it in abundance within yourself. About approval, approve yourself first and it won't matter who disapproves of you. This is so that you can want things to complement the life you already have and not need them to complete you. This is what strong minded people do; they want things, but they do not need them.

ii.   *Use logic to balance your emotions*

Being human, we have been given a gift - the ability to feel things; we have emotions. They have a strong hold on us and they have the power to lift us and also to take down even the best of us. Love, fear, anxiety, anger are all emotions – and they have build and destroyed lives.

How many dumb things have you done for love, which you wouldn't do even under the influence? How many times have you let things happen, which you did not like all because you were afraid?

Emotions control us.

When you are mentally strong, you understand that emotions can influence your thinking – and drive you to make stupid decisions. Therefore, you should learn not to let yourself become an emotional ball, reacting and making decisions based on how you are feeling in the moment.

Before you make decisions, confront your emotions with logic. You see, logic acts from a place of validity or reasonability. It involves the rational mind which is evaluative in nature; it accesses a mater from all angles and asks the "why" "what" and "how" questions before making a conclusion.

iii. Stop taking everything personally

Manipulators really love people who take things personally – they can get through their mental and emotional walls easily and make you suffer with just a small attack.

Someone is in a bad mood, and you are thinking "what could I have done to trigger this?'. You start to blame yourself and even apologize for things you did not do. You have made it about you – and they will ride on this tide.

A strong mind knows better than to take everything personally. You see a lot that happens in life; in our environment, to us or with people we love is completely impersonal. We like to make it about us, but really, it has nothing to do with us – it's not about you!

For instance, you could be blaming yourself for a friendship or relationship that's on the rocks. When you step back, maybe after you take a break from it, you will realize that you have been missing pointers of the real cause of the problems - which could be the other person's behavior.

Free yourself from this trap and stop inviting suffering. Always take time to step back and see things from a spectator's perspective. You will see that much of what has been happening, things you have made yourself suffer over, really has nothing to do with you.

iv. Learn to be responsible for only that you can control and accept what you can't change

A strong minded individual knows how to be responsible, but they do not take responsibility for everything. They accept the fact that there are things that are out of their control and trying to control such would only lead to suffering. Such things include; other people (their actions, reactions and moods), the weather and even circumstances. They will accept these as they are and quickly detach their emotions from it.

>   v. *Be flexible enough to accept change*

A strong mind is open to the possibility that things and people change. For this reason, change does not catch them off guard and topple their emotions. You see, change is inevitable; it's the only constant that we have in this world.

To be prepared for change is to be prepared to live. In relationships, you will know when it's time to let things be or when to walk away – and you will not hesitate to. Fear of change will no longer hold you back.

>   vi. *Build mental and emotional strength against negativity*

As long as you are in this world, there is no way to avoid negativity. It will come to you from different directions; from within and also from external factors. There will be negative feelings and thoughts from within you and there will also be negative people with negative feedback, energies and circumstances. For instance, a blackmailing individual in your life is one of those negative people – and it could be a family member, hard to eliminate.

Learn to identify and challenge negative thoughts and deal with the negative feelings – without ignoring or suppressing them. When it comes to negative people and their ideas or feedback, you need to learn to not take it personally or take it to heart because it is only when you give it mental space that it will affect you. Let them spread their negativity however much they can, because there is little you can do to make them not to. However, don't ever let it get to you; do not engage. If possible, minimize your contact with them or eliminate them from your life.

Develop Boundaries

Do you have boundaries? Do any exist within your relationships? You see, many people believe the popularly traded lie (especially by narcissists and their likes) that having boundaries is similar to being an aloof person – secretive and distant. This is not true; if you encounter anyone believing in that and who gets mad because you have boundaries, beware of their motive.

To have boundaries basically means that you know what you like, what you accept and are very clear about what you can tolerate. It means that you have or are aware of deal breakers in every area of your life; not everything is 'just okay'. It also means that you have beliefs, values, standards and limits that guide your choices and decisions. To have boundaries means that you are able to communicate clearly what you want and what you do not want and recognizing that not everyone will agree with this, but you stand your ground regardless.

Boundaries help you to protect what you deem important. Also, they help to preserve your energy, mental space and time for only the things that matter to you; you do not have to over exert yourself. More importantly, they set a limit for how far people can get involved/interfere in your affairs; they set a stop sign that says "hey, this is the farthest you can go, thank you". It is your boundaries that teach people how they should treat you.

Signs Of Lack Of Or Weak Boundaries

- You are feeling responsible for how other people feel. You are constantly worried about if they are happy, contented, having a good time and so on and when they are sad, you think it's your duty to make them happy. Some would say that this is very noble of you but this 'noble duty' means that you are anxious and guilty most of the time.

- You are not satisfied with the way you are living your life; it feels like you never get to do the things you want to do. This is because most of the time, you are going along with others; following their schedules and getting trapped in their plans. Mostly this is because…

- You are afraid to let others down - and so you would rather let you down. This means that you abandon your plans, ditch your values and lower your standards if you have to, to go along with others.

- You think that people do not respect you, because they don't seem to attach any importance to your opinions, stay out of your affairs or have respect for your time or things you want to do.

- It feels like you don't really know who you are or what love doing, like you have an identity crisis when you are left alone. This is because you spend most of your time tagging along people and living their life.

- You feel as if people close to you are taking advantage of you – to a point that you wonder if being close to people means serving them and neglecting you.

Are these experiences you have been having? You lack boundaries which is the reason why you are easy to blackmail or take advantage off. You need some boundaries; let's teach you how to establish them.

How To Establish Boundaries

Step one: Become aware of how you feel and what is important to you

These are the guidelines of boundaries; how you feel about things and also the things that are important to you.

- **Use a journal** to write down your experiences of the day, the events, and the people you met and so on. Write about how they made you feel - and remember you don't have to pretend here; you can be real with your journal. Jot down the sensations, frustrations, the joys and all those feelings that you felt say, while hanging out in a certain place or with certain people.

    Next, write about what you derive from those experiences; what lessons did you learn? It could be that you went out to a club because your friend had you tag along but you ended up feeling so uncomfortable, like you are out of place. Here, you learn that those noisy places with flashy lights are not your 'thing'.

After a while, as you reread what you have been writing, you will start to notice patterns and themes around things or people that make you happy, angry or frustrated – and you will know what or whom to allow in and determine how far it goes.

- **Meditation**: it brings you to a deep level of consciousness whereby you are aware of feelings and sensations in your body in the present moment. You are able to observe your mind and notice patterns. This is a practice that helps you bring your deepest feelings (which are uncorrupted and true) to the surface.

This step enables you to be in tune with who you are and how you feel which helps you identify what you want and what you do not want in your life.

Step 2: Know your limits

Guided by step one above, you know where to draw the lines. Now, you need to clearly define your boundaries with people close to you (family, friends, intimate partners, work colleagues) and strangers alike. Your past experiences with people not forgetting activities you have been involved in and how they made you feel will help you know where to draw the line.

You see, in experiences where you felt uncomfortable, angry, frustrated or lost, it could be that these feelings arose because your boundaries were crossed; those feelings were meant to tell you what you are not comfortable with.

Now, use those experiences and set limits with people. A boundary chart where you fill in the type of boundaries in each relationship with brief descriptions of the boundary should be a good place to start. For instance, "I don't like it when my partner monitors my every move". In future, you can use this information to assess when a person may be overstepping.

Step 3: Put the boundaries into practice

It's time to start applying the boundaries in your life and relationships. Mind you, not everyone is going to be happy with the fact that now you have limits –especially if they were used to taking advantage of you. Your boundaries may result in negative consequences for some relationships. It's only normal that a person whom you have always said yes to hears 'no' for the first time. They will rebel against you and probably say that you have 'changed' hoping that you will back down and become the little old 'nice' you who gave in to their demands. This is why if you want them boundaries to stay in place and to be respected; you need to be clear and consistent about them. The following tips will help you execute this step;

How To Make Your Boundaries Stand

i. Learn to say them out loud

It may take a little practice, assuming you were never used to saying 'no' to people, but you need to start somewhere - and now.

How do you say it?

A neutral tone will do; it brings you off as calm and certain – not a person who is trying to put on an act of bravery.

What do you say?

You need to carefully construct what you are going to say, so as to clearly and firmly communicate to the other person about crossing a boundary. A good message would be made of these three parts:

- A reference to the act in question; what happened. Be careful not to make a personal attack; avoid saying "you did…" Instead, refer to the specific at or behavior.
- Mention your boundary regarding such actions/behavior and how you feel about it.

- Tell them the alternative behavior, which you are okay with to guide them on what you would expect in future

An example of direct communication of a boundary: "That kind of behavior makes me feel really upset. I don't believe in doing things in such a manner. In the future, I would appreciate it if you (accepted behavior).

An indirect/friendly but precise communication: "I really appreciate that you included me in your plans for (an activity). I don't have time to do that right now. However, I would really love to do that with you sometime. Please let me know in advance when you are doing (activity) next and maybe I could make time.

ii. *Have some coping statements ready – for you*

Sometimes, your communication of a boundary will evoke reactions you do not like from people. For instance, a friend may start to behave as if you let them down so bad or a partner may be sad because of your refusal. And then you will think to yourself "I could take it this once just for them". The truth is, you will always 'do it for them' time and again because this is how they will always react.

When you find yourself about to cave in to give in to demands, have a coping statement in your head to keep you on course. For instance, "Their reaction is not my business. I have a responsibility to preserve my peace, time and values"

iii. *Stand your ground*

When you set a boundary with a person, you need to stay put; no compromise and no negotiations. Do not try to reason with them about it; this is negotiating your boundaries and it makes you look like you are not sure or serious about them. Not even a tear or tantrum should make you waver; fight to stand your ground so that there are no mixed messages. This is the only way that they can understand that you mean what you say and that no amount of pressure is going to make you give in.

iv. Learn to soothe yourself

It can be scary to learn to talk back when you are used to backing down and letting people get their way. In the beginning, when you stand your ground, your flight or fight response, which is the body's response to stressful situation, will be turned on. Standing by your boundaries in the face of a person who is used to having their way and is bent on keeping it that way is going to be scary.

Turn off the flight of fight response with self-soothing exercises such as deep breathing. They will keep you calm and help keep your tone normal and neutral so that they do not sense fear or anxiety in you – and use it against you.

v. Be assertive

Follow through on maintaining your boundaries. Do not be quiet like you used to be and let people step all over you. You already know your limits; take it upon you to remind people who cross them that they are in forbidden territory. This does not mean that you are being rude or unkind; you are simply being honest and fair while protecting yourself – and eliminating misunderstandings.

How To Handle A Blackmail Situation And The Blackmailer In The Moment

We have discussed about how you can work on yourself to make yourself stronger and more resistant to blackmail. Now it's time to put the blackmailer in their place; keep in mind that you cannot change them but you can let them know that you are not going to tolerate their behavior, can't you?

Also, it is important to remember that this kind of blackmail is targeting your emotions, which are very powerful parts of us, and they may take a hit and cause us to react as the perpetrator intended. This is why you need to know how to respond in the moment of blackmail to protect your emotions so that they (the blackmailer) do not have a chance of succeeding.

i. Practice detached observation

This means that you avoid getting too emotionally or mentally involved with the emotionally charged situation. Take a step back and watch what is happening as an observer would, without being carried away by the emotions.

Becoming a detached observer allows you time and space for self-refraction in order to make connections between what is going on, what is expected of you and your beliefs and values. This guides you to making informed and healthier decisions.

ii. Develop non-defensive communication to de-escalate the conflict

The blackmailer will make an unreasonable demand, and the victim will refuse them. The perpetrator will apply pressure and the victim responds with even more resistance. This creates an escalated conflict; blackmail usually thrives on conflict and escalation, one person gaining power over the other.

It is only natural to get defensive when you feel attacked. However, it does not get you far in a conflict; defensiveness breed defensiveness. You will tell them why they are being unreasonable or unfair and they will defend themselves, telling you how reasonable and appropriate their demands are and this will go on and on. You can never win by being defensive.

Non-defensive responses help you shift the dynamic and flatten the tide of conflict the blackmailer is riding on. They are statements used to protect you rather than defend you.

Non-Defensive Communication Skills

- Disengage from a defensive position; stop defending your opinion/idea/argument and maybe check into theirs. Let them see that you are interested in understanding them with statements such as, "Will you tell me why this is so important to you?".

- Empathize and disarm them: show them that you understand where they are coming from using statements such as; "I see where you are coming from, and you could be right. However I am feeling…"

- Focus on the issue at hand: stop addressing each other's opinions, focus on the issue. For instance if you feel disrespected say, " we need to find better ways to handle our issues in a way that we do not get to disrespecting each other" .

- Disclose personal needs and goals in a non-defensive manner: use statements such as "I am not willing to live like this anymore. I want to be happy, to feel respected and cared for. I want us to find ways to make each other feel more loved."

- Depersonalize issues: include the other person; if there is anything to be gained, let it be 'for us". For example, "these issues are pushing our relationship towards an edge of a cliff…"

Additional Tips In Handling Blackmail On The Spot

- Ask for time: Do not respond immediately; say to be given time to think about it. It will give you a break from the emotionally charged situation and give you time to assess and weigh the demand using logic.

- A neutral statement as the best answer for a demand: Avoid over-explaining yourself and trying to reason with them. Understand that they are not interested in other view point, just what they want. The back and forth will do nothing but to put more pressure and heat on the emotional exchange. Use a neutral statement for refusal; "no thank you, "no, I am sorry" are good examples to use.

- Pause before complying: even when it feels like the demand is reasonable, with a blackmailer, you never know. They could be using their tricks to make you believe so. Therefore, pause. Before you say yes, pause and process.

- Stand up for yourself now: stop complying, waiting until the day you get stronger, perhaps more courageous and less anxious or fearful to say no. Many have waited for this but it never really happens until you learn to act, even when afraid. Resist. Do it now and let the feelings catch up. Act with courage and you will start to feel courageous.

- Confront them: Call them out on their behavior. They need to know that it's unacceptable and you are not willing tolerate it anymore. Of course, you should make it non-defensive if you are not looking to escalate the confrontation. Also, make firm statements, addressing the behavior without beating around the bush explaining why you do not like it; you don't like it and you won't tolerate it, period! You need statements such as; "Hey, I am not sure what is going on here, but I will not tolerate you speaking to me like that anymore. If you are trying to tell me something, state it clearly so I may understand.

The Final Card

You have made yourself stronger, worked on your responses and you have tried to handle this person in the best way you could. However, for some reason, they have refused to change – and they won't even accept that their behavior is toxic. Despite you trying to make your boundaries clear, they won't stop overstepping them; they want to continue controlling you.

What are you going to do?

You have one final card to play

Do you owe them anything? If yes, settle everything with them; deliver your promise and meet your responsibilities. When that's done, remove yourself from the equation. What if they are family? You still will remain to be family but you can distance yourself from them and their affairs – they can't be too close because they will still use you. No relationship is worth your emotional and mental wellbeing. None is worth you losing the reigns of your life over.

Remove yourself to destabilize the blackmail equation. You see, for blackmail to work, there has to be four factors; the blackmailer, the victim and the demand. You are the victim; remove yourself. The blackmailer will be left with their demands but with no one to place them on. Game over!

Conclusion

Emotional blackmail succeeds only where there is a willing victim. Refuse to be that victim. You can do nothing to change the blackmailer, so work on improving yourself. A wise man said, "Do not blame a clown for being a clown; ask yourself why you keep going to the circus". So, don't be mad because they are blackmailers; ask yourself what you can do to stop being someone they can prey on. This book just told you what to do; start now!

FANTON PUBLISHERS
FANTONPUBLISHERS.COM

THANK YOU

Do You Like My Book & Approach To Publishing?

If you like my writing and style and would love the ease of learning literally everything you can get your hands on from Fantonpublishers.com, I'd really need you to do me either of the following favors.

1: First, I'd Love It If You Leave a Review of This Book on Amazon.

2: Check Out My Emotional Mastery Books

Emotional Intelligence: The Mindfulness Guide To Mastering Your Emotions, Getting Ahead And Improving Your Life

Narcissist: How To Neutralize A Narcissist: A Complete Guide on How to Become a Narcissist's Worst Nightmare

Stress: The Psychology of Managing Pressure: Practical Strategies to turn Pressure into Positive Energy (5 Key Stress Techniques for Stress, Anxiety, and Depression Relief)

Failure Is Not The END: It Is An Emotional Gym: Complete Workout Plan On How To Build Your Emotional Muscle And Burning Down Anxiety To Become Emotionally Stronger, More Confident and Less Reactive

Subconscious Mind: Tame, Reprogram & Control Your Subconscious Mind To Transform Your Life

Body Language: Master Body Language: A Practical Guide to Understanding Nonverbal Communication and Improving Your Relationships

Shame and Guilt: Overcoming Shame and Guilt: Step By Step Guide On How to Overcome Shame and Guilt for Good

Anger Management: A Simple Guide on How to Deal with Anger

Get updates when we publish any book that will help you master your emotions: http://bit.ly/2fantonpubpersonaldevl

To get a list of all my other books, please visit fantonpublishers, my author central or let me send you the list by requesting them below: http://bit.ly/2fantonpubnewbooks

3: Grab Some Freebies On Your Way Out; Giving Is Receiving, Right?

I gave you a complimentary book at the start of the book. If you are still interested, grab it here.

5 Pillar Life Transformation Checklist: http://bit.ly/2fantonfreebie

Printed in Great Britain
by Amazon